THIS BOOK BELONGS TO:

CONTACT INFORMATION	
NAME	
ADDRESS	
PHONE #	
EMAIL	

Dedication

This Budget Planner Notebook is dedicated to people who want to plan a budget, keep accurate records for finances, and organize yearly expenses.

You are my inspiration for producing this book and I'm honored to be a part of helping you manage and retain important information regarding your finances.

HOW TO USE THIS BOOK

This Budget Planner Notebook will help you record, collect, and organize your information in an easy to use format.

Here are examples of information for you to fill in and write the details for your budget activities.

Fill in the following information:

1. Yearly Summary - record monthly income, bill expenses, other expenses, saving and total for each month, then fill in yearly summary- budgeted and actual expenses

2. Monthly Budget - record month, budgeted amount, income (source 1, 2 other income), the total amount of income, record- bills to be paid, due date, the amount paid, the date paid, and the total

3. Monthly Budget - record other expenses, date, amount, and total

4. Weekly Expenses - record month, week, budget, track expenses Monday through Sunday, space for notes

YEARLY SUMMARY

YEAR:______

SUMMARY	BUDGETED	ACTUAL
INCOME		
BILL EXPENSES		
OTHER EXPENSES		
SAVINGS		
TOTAL		

JANUARY	FEBRUARY	MARCH
INCOME:	INCOME:	INCOME:
BILL EXPENSES:	BILL EXPENSES:	BILL EXPENSES:
OTHER EXPENSES:	OTHER EXPENSES:	OTHER EXPENSES:
SAVINGS:	SAVINGS:	SAVINGS:
TOTAL:	TOTAL:	TOTAL:
APRIL	**MAY**	**JUNE**
INCOME:	INCOME:	INCOME:
BILL EXPENSES:	BILL EXPENSES:	BILL EXPENSES:
OTHER EXPENSES:	OTHER EXPENSES:	OTHER EXPENSES:
SAVINGS:	SAVINGS:	SAVINGS:
TOTAL:	TOTAL:	TOTAL:
JULY	**AUGUST**	**SEPTEMBER**
INCOME:	INCOME:	INCOME:
BILL EXPENSES:	BILL EXPENSES:	BILL EXPENSES:
OTHER EXPENSES:	OTHER EXPENSES:	OTHER EXPENSES:
SAVINGS:	SAVINGS:	SAVINGS:
TOTAL:	TOTAL:	TOTAL:
OCTOBER	**NOVEMBER**	**DECEMBER**
INCOME:	INCOME:	INCOME:
BILL EXPENSES:	BILL EXPENSES:	BILL EXPENSES:
OTHER EXPENSES:	OTHER EXPENSES:	OTHER EXPENSES:
SAVINGS:	SAVINGS:	SAVINGS:
TOTAL:	TOTAL:	TOTAL:

MONTHLY BUDGET

MONTH:__________________ **BUDGET:**_______________

INCOME		AMOUNT
SOURCE 1:		
SOURCE 2:		
OTHER INCOME:		
	TOTAL	

BILLS TO BE PAID	DATE DUE	AMOUNT	PAID
	TOTAL		

MONTHLY BUDGET

OTHER EXPENSES	DATE	AMOUNT

TOTAL	

TOTAL INCOME	TOTAL EXPENSES	DIFFERENCE

WEEKLY EXPENSES

MONTH:__________ WEEK:_________ BUDGET: _________

MONDAY

DESCRIPTION	AMOUNT
TOTAL	

TUESDAY

DESCRIPTION	AMOUNT
TOTAL	

WEDNESDAY

DESCRIPTION	AMOUNT
TOTAL	

THURSDAY

DESCRIPTION	AMOUNT
TOTAL	

WEEKLY EXPENSES

FRIDAY

DESCRIPTION	AMOUNT
TOTAL	

SATURDAY

DESCRIPTION	AMOUNT
TOTAL	

SUNDAY

DESCRIPTION	AMOUNT
TOTAL	

NOTES

WEEKLY EXPENSES

MONTH:__________ WEEK:_________ BUDGET: _________

MONDAY

DESCRIPTION	AMOUNT
TOTAL	

TUESDAY

DESCRIPTION	AMOUNT
TOTAL	

WEDNESDAY

DESCRIPTION	AMOUNT
TOTAL	

THURSDAY

DESCRIPTION	AMOUNT
TOTAL	

WEEKLY EXPENSES

FRIDAY

DESCRIPTION	AMOUNT
TOTAL	

SATURDAY

DESCRIPTION	AMOUNT
TOTAL	

SUNDAY

DESCRIPTION	AMOUNT
TOTAL	

NOTES

WEEKLY EXPENSES

MONTH:__________ WEEK:_________ BUDGET: _________

MONDAY

DESCRIPTION	AMOUNT
TOTAL	

TUESDAY

DESCRIPTION	AMOUNT
TOTAL	

WEDNESDAY

DESCRIPTION	AMOUNT
TOTAL	

THURSDAY

DESCRIPTION	AMOUNT
TOTAL	

WEEKLY EXPENSES

FRIDAY

DESCRIPTION	AMOUNT
TOTAL	

SATURDAY

DESCRIPTION	AMOUNT
TOTAL	

SUNDAY

DESCRIPTION	AMOUNT
TOTAL	

NOTES

WEEKLY EXPENSES

MONTH:__________ WEEK:_________ BUDGET: _________

MONDAY

DESCRIPTION	AMOUNT
TOTAL	

TUESDAY

DESCRIPTION	AMOUNT
TOTAL	

WEDNESDAY

DESCRIPTION	AMOUNT
TOTAL	

THURSDAY

DESCRIPTION	AMOUNT
TOTAL	

WEEKLY EXPENSES

FRIDAY

DESCRIPTION	AMOUNT
TOTAL	

SATURDAY

DESCRIPTION	AMOUNT
TOTAL	

SUNDAY

DESCRIPTION	AMOUNT
TOTAL	

NOTES

MONTHLY BUDGET

MONTH:__________________ **BUDGET:_______________**

INCOME		AMOUNT
SOURCE 1:		
SOURCE 2:		
OTHER INCOME:		
	TOTAL	

BILLS TO BE PAID	DATE DUE	AMOUNT	PAID
	TOTAL		

MONTHLY BUDGET

OTHER EXPENSES	DATE	AMOUNT
TOTAL		

TOTAL INCOME	TOTAL EXPENSES	DIFFERENCE

WEEKLY EXPENSES

MONTH:__________ WEEK:_________ BUDGET: _________

MONDAY

DESCRIPTION	AMOUNT
TOTAL	

TUESDAY

DESCRIPTION	AMOUNT
TOTAL	

WEDNESDAY

DESCRIPTION	AMOUNT
TOTAL	

THURSDAY

DESCRIPTION	AMOUNT
TOTAL	

WEEKLY EXPENSES

FRIDAY

DESCRIPTION	AMOUNT
TOTAL	

SATURDAY

DESCRIPTION	AMOUNT
TOTAL	

SUNDAY

DESCRIPTION	AMOUNT
TOTAL	

NOTES

WEEKLY EXPENSES

MONTH:__________ WEEK:_________ BUDGET: _________

MONDAY

DESCRIPTION	AMOUNT
TOTAL	

TUESDAY

DESCRIPTION	AMOUNT
TOTAL	

WEDNESDAY

DESCRIPTION	AMOUNT
TOTAL	

THURSDAY

DESCRIPTION	AMOUNT
TOTAL	

WEEKLY EXPENSES

FRIDAY

DESCRIPTION	AMOUNT
TOTAL	

SATURDAY

DESCRIPTION	AMOUNT
TOTAL	

SUNDAY

DESCRIPTION	AMOUNT
TOTAL	

NOTES

WEEKLY EXPENSES

MONTH:__________ WEEK:_________ BUDGET: _________

MONDAY

DESCRIPTION	AMOUNT
TOTAL	

TUESDAY

DESCRIPTION	AMOUNT
TOTAL	

WEDNESDAY

DESCRIPTION	AMOUNT
TOTAL	

THURSDAY

DESCRIPTION	AMOUNT
TOTAL	

WEEKLY EXPENSES

FRIDAY

DESCRIPTION	AMOUNT
TOTAL	

SATURDAY

DESCRIPTION	AMOUNT
TOTAL	

SUNDAY

DESCRIPTION	AMOUNT
TOTAL	

NOTES

WEEKLY EXPENSES

MONTH:__________ WEEK:_________ BUDGET: _________

MONDAY

DESCRIPTION	AMOUNT
TOTAL	

TUESDAY

DESCRIPTION	AMOUNT
TOTAL	

WEDNESDAY

DESCRIPTION	AMOUNT
TOTAL	

THURSDAY

DESCRIPTION	AMOUNT
TOTAL	

WEEKLY EXPENSES

FRIDAY

DESCRIPTION	AMOUNT
TOTAL	

SATURDAY

DESCRIPTION	AMOUNT
TOTAL	

SUNDAY

DESCRIPTION	AMOUNT
TOTAL	

NOTES

MONTHLY BUDGET

MONTH: ________________ **BUDGET:** ______________

INCOME	AMOUNT
SOURCE 1:	
SOURCE 2:	
OTHER INCOME:	
TOTAL	

BILLS TO BE PAID	DATE DUE	AMOUNT	PAID
	TOTAL		

MONTHLY BUDGET

OTHER EXPENSES	DATE	AMOUNT
TOTAL		

TOTAL INCOME	TOTAL EXPENSES	DIFFERENCE

WEEKLY EXPENSES

MONTH:__________ WEEK:_________ BUDGET: _________

MONDAY

DESCRIPTION	AMOUNT
TOTAL	

TUESDAY

DESCRIPTION	AMOUNT
TOTAL	

WEDNESDAY

DESCRIPTION	AMOUNT
TOTAL	

THURSDAY

DESCRIPTION	AMOUNT
TOTAL	

WEEKLY EXPENSES

FRIDAY

DESCRIPTION	AMOUNT
TOTAL	

SATURDAY

DESCRIPTION	AMOUNT
TOTAL	

SUNDAY

DESCRIPTION	AMOUNT
TOTAL	

NOTES

WEEKLY EXPENSES

MONTH:__________ WEEK:_________ BUDGET: _________

MONDAY

DESCRIPTION	AMOUNT
TOTAL	

TUESDAY

DESCRIPTION	AMOUNT
TOTAL	

WEDNESDAY

DESCRIPTION	AMOUNT
TOTAL	

THURSDAY

DESCRIPTION	AMOUNT
TOTAL	

WEEKLY EXPENSES

FRIDAY

DESCRIPTION	AMOUNT
TOTAL	

SATURDAY

DESCRIPTION	AMOUNT
TOTAL	

SUNDAY

DESCRIPTION	AMOUNT
TOTAL	

NOTES

WEEKLY EXPENSES

MONTH:__________ WEEK:_________ BUDGET: _________

MONDAY

DESCRIPTION	AMOUNT
TOTAL	

TUESDAY

DESCRIPTION	AMOUNT
TOTAL	

WEDNESDAY

DESCRIPTION	AMOUNT
TOTAL	

THURSDAY

DESCRIPTION	AMOUNT
TOTAL	

WEEKLY EXPENSES

FRIDAY

DESCRIPTION	AMOUNT
TOTAL	

SATURDAY

DESCRIPTION	AMOUNT
TOTAL	

SUNDAY

DESCRIPTION	AMOUNT
TOTAL	

NOTES

WEEKLY EXPENSES

MONTH:__________ WEEK:_________ BUDGET: _________

MONDAY

DESCRIPTION	AMOUNT
TOTAL	

TUESDAY

DESCRIPTION	AMOUNT
TOTAL	

WEDNESDAY

DESCRIPTION	AMOUNT
TOTAL	

THURSDAY

DESCRIPTION	AMOUNT
TOTAL	

WEEKLY EXPENSES

FRIDAY

DESCRIPTION	AMOUNT
TOTAL	

SATURDAY

DESCRIPTION	AMOUNT
TOTAL	

SUNDAY

DESCRIPTION	AMOUNT
TOTAL	

NOTES

MONTHLY BUDGET

MONTH:__________________ **BUDGET:**______________

INCOME	AMOUNT
SOURCE 1:	
SOURCE 2:	
OTHER INCOME:	
TOTAL	

BILLS TO BE PAID	DATE DUE	AMOUNT	PAID
	TOTAL		

MONTHLY BUDGET

OTHER EXPENSES	DATE	AMOUNT
TOTAL		

TOTAL INCOME	TOTAL EXPENSES	DIFFERENCE

WEEKLY EXPENSES

MONTH:__________ WEEK:_________ BUDGET: _________

MONDAY

DESCRIPTION	AMOUNT
TOTAL	

TUESDAY

DESCRIPTION	AMOUNT
TOTAL	

WEDNESDAY

DESCRIPTION	AMOUNT
TOTAL	

THURSDAY

DESCRIPTION	AMOUNT
TOTAL	

WEEKLY EXPENSES

FRIDAY

DESCRIPTION	AMOUNT
TOTAL	

SATURDAY

DESCRIPTION	AMOUNT
TOTAL	

SUNDAY

DESCRIPTION	AMOUNT
TOTAL	

NOTES

WEEKLY EXPENSES

MONTH:__________ WEEK:_________ BUDGET: _________

MONDAY

DESCRIPTION	AMOUNT
TOTAL	

TUESDAY

DESCRIPTION	AMOUNT
TOTAL	

WEDNESDAY

DESCRIPTION	AMOUNT
TOTAL	

THURSDAY

DESCRIPTION	AMOUNT
TOTAL	

WEEKLY EXPENSES

FRIDAY

DESCRIPTION	AMOUNT
TOTAL	

SATURDAY

DESCRIPTION	AMOUNT
TOTAL	

SUNDAY

DESCRIPTION	AMOUNT
TOTAL	

NOTES

WEEKLY EXPENSES

MONTH:__________ WEEK:_________ BUDGET: _________

MONDAY

DESCRIPTION	AMOUNT
TOTAL	

TUESDAY

DESCRIPTION	AMOUNT
TOTAL	

WEDNESDAY

DESCRIPTION	AMOUNT
TOTAL	

THURSDAY

DESCRIPTION	AMOUNT
TOTAL	

WEEKLY EXPENSES

FRIDAY

DESCRIPTION	AMOUNT
TOTAL	

SATURDAY

DESCRIPTION	AMOUNT
TOTAL	

SUNDAY

DESCRIPTION	AMOUNT
TOTAL	

NOTES

WEEKLY EXPENSES

MONTH:__________ WEEK:_________ BUDGET: _________

MONDAY

DESCRIPTION	AMOUNT
TOTAL	

TUESDAY

DESCRIPTION	AMOUNT
TOTAL	

WEDNESDAY

DESCRIPTION	AMOUNT
TOTAL	

THURSDAY

DESCRIPTION	AMOUNT
TOTAL	

WEEKLY EXPENSES

FRIDAY

DESCRIPTION	AMOUNT
TOTAL	

SATURDAY

DESCRIPTION	AMOUNT
TOTAL	

SUNDAY

DESCRIPTION	AMOUNT
TOTAL	

NOTES

MONTHLY BUDGET

MONTH:__________________ BUDGET:_______________

INCOME	AMOUNT
SOURCE 1:	
SOURCE 2:	
OTHER INCOME:	
TOTAL	

BILLS TO BE PAID	DATE DUE	AMOUNT	PAID
	TOTAL		

MONTHLY BUDGET

OTHER EXPENSES	DATE	AMOUNT
TOTAL		

TOTAL INCOME	TOTAL EXPENSES	DIFFERENCE

WEEKLY EXPENSES

MONTH:__________ WEEK:_________ BUDGET: _________

MONDAY

DESCRIPTION	AMOUNT
TOTAL	

TUESDAY

DESCRIPTION	AMOUNT
TOTAL	

WEDNESDAY

DESCRIPTION	AMOUNT
TOTAL	

THURSDAY

DESCRIPTION	AMOUNT
TOTAL	

WEEKLY EXPENSES

FRIDAY

DESCRIPTION	AMOUNT
TOTAL	

SATURDAY

DESCRIPTION	AMOUNT
TOTAL	

SUNDAY

DESCRIPTION	AMOUNT
TOTAL	

NOTES

WEEKLY EXPENSES

MONTH:__________ WEEK:_________ BUDGET: _________

MONDAY

DESCRIPTION	AMOUNT
TOTAL	

TUESDAY

DESCRIPTION	AMOUNT
TOTAL	

WEDNESDAY

DESCRIPTION	AMOUNT
TOTAL	

THURSDAY

DESCRIPTION	AMOUNT
TOTAL	

WEEKLY EXPENSES

FRIDAY

DESCRIPTION	AMOUNT
TOTAL	

SATURDAY

DESCRIPTION	AMOUNT
TOTAL	

SUNDAY

DESCRIPTION	AMOUNT
TOTAL	

NOTES

WEEKLY EXPENSES

MONTH:__________ WEEK:_________ BUDGET: _________

MONDAY

DESCRIPTION	AMOUNT
TOTAL	

TUESDAY

DESCRIPTION	AMOUNT
TOTAL	

WEDNESDAY

DESCRIPTION	AMOUNT
TOTAL	

THURSDAY

DESCRIPTION	AMOUNT
TOTAL	

WEEKLY EXPENSES

FRIDAY

DESCRIPTION	AMOUNT
TOTAL	

SATURDAY

DESCRIPTION	AMOUNT
TOTAL	

SUNDAY

DESCRIPTION	AMOUNT
TOTAL	

NOTES

WEEKLY EXPENSES

MONTH:__________ WEEK:_________ BUDGET: _________

MONDAY

DESCRIPTION	AMOUNT
TOTAL	

TUESDAY

DESCRIPTION	AMOUNT
TOTAL	

WEDNESDAY

DESCRIPTION	AMOUNT
TOTAL	

THURSDAY

DESCRIPTION	AMOUNT
TOTAL	

WEEKLY EXPENSES

FRIDAY

DESCRIPTION	AMOUNT
TOTAL	

SATURDAY

DESCRIPTION	AMOUNT
TOTAL	

SUNDAY

DESCRIPTION	AMOUNT
TOTAL	

NOTES

MONTHLY BUDGET

MONTH:________________ **BUDGET:**______________

INCOME	AMOUNT
SOURCE 1:	
SOURCE 2:	
OTHER INCOME:	
TOTAL	

BILLS TO BE PAID	DATE DUE	AMOUNT	PAID
	TOTAL		

MONTHLY BUDGET

OTHER EXPENSES	DATE	AMOUNT
TOTAL		

TOTAL INCOME	TOTAL EXPENSES	DIFFERENCE

WEEKLY EXPENSES

MONTH:__________ WEEK:_________ BUDGET: _________

MONDAY

DESCRIPTION	AMOUNT
TOTAL	

TUESDAY

DESCRIPTION	AMOUNT
TOTAL	

WEDNESDAY

DESCRIPTION	AMOUNT
TOTAL	

THURSDAY

DESCRIPTION	AMOUNT
TOTAL	

WEEKLY EXPENSES

FRIDAY

DESCRIPTION	AMOUNT
TOTAL	

SATURDAY

DESCRIPTION	AMOUNT
TOTAL	

SUNDAY

DESCRIPTION	AMOUNT
TOTAL	

NOTES

WEEKLY EXPENSES

MONTH:__________ WEEK:_________ BUDGET: _________

MONDAY

DESCRIPTION	AMOUNT
TOTAL	

TUESDAY

DESCRIPTION	AMOUNT
TOTAL	

WEDNESDAY

DESCRIPTION	AMOUNT
TOTAL	

THURSDAY

DESCRIPTION	AMOUNT
TOTAL	

WEEKLY EXPENSES

FRIDAY

DESCRIPTION	AMOUNT
TOTAL	

SATURDAY

DESCRIPTION	AMOUNT
TOTAL	

SUNDAY

DESCRIPTION	AMOUNT
TOTAL	

NOTES

WEEKLY EXPENSES

MONTH:__________ WEEK:_________ BUDGET: _________

MONDAY

DESCRIPTION	AMOUNT
TOTAL	

TUESDAY

DESCRIPTION	AMOUNT
TOTAL	

WEDNESDAY

DESCRIPTION	AMOUNT
TOTAL	

THURSDAY

DESCRIPTION	AMOUNT
TOTAL	

WEEKLY EXPENSES

FRIDAY

DESCRIPTION	AMOUNT
TOTAL	

SATURDAY

DESCRIPTION	AMOUNT
TOTAL	

SUNDAY

DESCRIPTION	AMOUNT
TOTAL	

NOTES

WEEKLY EXPENSES

MONTH:__________ WEEK:_________ BUDGET: _________

MONDAY

DESCRIPTION	AMOUNT
TOTAL	

TUESDAY

DESCRIPTION	AMOUNT
TOTAL	

WEDNESDAY

DESCRIPTION	AMOUNT
TOTAL	

THURSDAY

DESCRIPTION	AMOUNT
TOTAL	

WEEKLY EXPENSES

FRIDAY

DESCRIPTION	AMOUNT
TOTAL	

SATURDAY

DESCRIPTION	AMOUNT
TOTAL	

SUNDAY

DESCRIPTION	AMOUNT
TOTAL	

NOTES

MONTHLY BUDGET

MONTH:__________________ **BUDGET:**_______________

INCOME		AMOUNT
SOURCE 1:		
SOURCE 2:		
OTHER INCOME:		
	TOTAL	

BILLS TO BE PAID	DATE DUE	AMOUNT	PAID
	TOTAL		

MONTHLY BUDGET

OTHER EXPENSES	DATE	AMOUNT
TOTAL		

TOTAL INCOME	TOTAL EXPENSES	DIFFERENCE

WEEKLY EXPENSES

MONTH:__________ WEEK:_________ BUDGET: _________

MONDAY

DESCRIPTION	AMOUNT
TOTAL	

TUESDAY

DESCRIPTION	AMOUNT
TOTAL	

WEDNESDAY

DESCRIPTION	AMOUNT
TOTAL	

THURSDAY

DESCRIPTION	AMOUNT
TOTAL	

WEEKLY EXPENSES

FRIDAY

DESCRIPTION	AMOUNT
TOTAL	

SATURDAY

DESCRIPTION	AMOUNT
TOTAL	

SUNDAY

DESCRIPTION	AMOUNT
TOTAL	

NOTES

WEEKLY EXPENSES

MONTH:__________ WEEK:_________ BUDGET: _________

MONDAY

DESCRIPTION	AMOUNT
TOTAL	

TUESDAY

DESCRIPTION	AMOUNT
TOTAL	

WEDNESDAY

DESCRIPTION	AMOUNT
TOTAL	

THURSDAY

DESCRIPTION	AMOUNT
TOTAL	

WEEKLY EXPENSES

FRIDAY

DESCRIPTION	AMOUNT
TOTAL	

SATURDAY

DESCRIPTION	AMOUNT
TOTAL	

SUNDAY

DESCRIPTION	AMOUNT
TOTAL	

NOTES

WEEKLY EXPENSES

MONTH:__________ WEEK:_________ BUDGET: _________

MONDAY

DESCRIPTION	AMOUNT
TOTAL	

TUESDAY

DESCRIPTION	AMOUNT
TOTAL	

WEDNESDAY

DESCRIPTION	AMOUNT
TOTAL	

THURSDAY

DESCRIPTION	AMOUNT
TOTAL	

WEEKLY EXPENSES

FRIDAY

DESCRIPTION	AMOUNT
TOTAL	

SATURDAY

DESCRIPTION	AMOUNT
TOTAL	

SUNDAY

DESCRIPTION	AMOUNT
TOTAL	

NOTES

WEEKLY EXPENSES

MONTH:__________ WEEK:_________ BUDGET: _________

MONDAY

DESCRIPTION	AMOUNT
TOTAL	

TUESDAY

DESCRIPTION	AMOUNT
TOTAL	

WEDNESDAY

DESCRIPTION	AMOUNT
TOTAL	

THURSDAY

DESCRIPTION	AMOUNT
TOTAL	

WEEKLY EXPENSES

FRIDAY

DESCRIPTION	AMOUNT
TOTAL	

SATURDAY

DESCRIPTION	AMOUNT
TOTAL	

SUNDAY

DESCRIPTION	AMOUNT
TOTAL	

NOTES

MONTHLY BUDGET

MONTH:__________________ **BUDGET:**_______________

INCOME		AMOUNT
SOURCE 1:		
SOURCE 2:		
OTHER INCOME:		
	TOTAL	

BILLS TO BE PAID	DATE DUE	AMOUNT	PAID
	TOTAL		

MONTHLY BUDGET

OTHER EXPENSES	DATE	AMOUNT
TOTAL		

TOTAL INCOME	TOTAL EXPENSES	DIFFERENCE

WEEKLY EXPENSES

MONTH:__________ WEEK:_________ BUDGET: _________

MONDAY

DESCRIPTION	AMOUNT
TOTAL	

TUESDAY

DESCRIPTION	AMOUNT
TOTAL	

WEDNESDAY

DESCRIPTION	AMOUNT
TOTAL	

THURSDAY

DESCRIPTION	AMOUNT
TOTAL	

WEEKLY EXPENSES

FRIDAY

DESCRIPTION	AMOUNT
TOTAL	

SATURDAY

DESCRIPTION	AMOUNT
TOTAL	

SUNDAY

DESCRIPTION	AMOUNT
TOTAL	

NOTES

WEEKLY EXPENSES

MONTH:__________ WEEK:_________ BUDGET: _________

MONDAY

DESCRIPTION	AMOUNT
TOTAL	

TUESDAY

DESCRIPTION	AMOUNT
TOTAL	

WEDNESDAY

DESCRIPTION	AMOUNT
TOTAL	

THURSDAY

DESCRIPTION	AMOUNT
TOTAL	

WEEKLY EXPENSES

FRIDAY

DESCRIPTION	AMOUNT
TOTAL	

SATURDAY

DESCRIPTION	AMOUNT
TOTAL	

SUNDAY

DESCRIPTION	AMOUNT
TOTAL	

NOTES

WEEKLY EXPENSES

MONTH:__________ WEEK:_________ BUDGET: _________

MONDAY

DESCRIPTION	AMOUNT
TOTAL	

TUESDAY

DESCRIPTION	AMOUNT
TOTAL	

WEDNESDAY

DESCRIPTION	AMOUNT
TOTAL	

THURSDAY

DESCRIPTION	AMOUNT
TOTAL	

WEEKLY EXPENSES

FRIDAY

DESCRIPTION	AMOUNT
TOTAL	

SATURDAY

DESCRIPTION	AMOUNT
TOTAL	

SUNDAY

DESCRIPTION	AMOUNT
TOTAL	

NOTES

WEEKLY EXPENSES

MONTH:__________ WEEK:_________ BUDGET: _________

MONDAY

DESCRIPTION	AMOUNT
TOTAL	

TUESDAY

DESCRIPTION	AMOUNT
TOTAL	

WEDNESDAY

DESCRIPTION	AMOUNT
TOTAL	

THURSDAY

DESCRIPTION	AMOUNT
TOTAL	

WEEKLY EXPENSES

FRIDAY

DESCRIPTION	AMOUNT
TOTAL	

SATURDAY

DESCRIPTION	AMOUNT
TOTAL	

SUNDAY

DESCRIPTION	AMOUNT
TOTAL	

NOTES

MONTHLY BUDGET

MONTH:__________________ BUDGET:_______________

INCOME	AMOUNT
SOURCE 1:	
SOURCE 2:	
OTHER INCOME:	
TOTAL	

BILLS TO BE PAID	DATE DUE	AMOUNT	PAID
	TOTAL		

MONTHLY BUDGET

OTHER EXPENSES	DATE	AMOUNT
TOTAL		

TOTAL INCOME	TOTAL EXPENSES	DIFFERENCE

WEEKLY EXPENSES

MONTH:__________ WEEK:_________ BUDGET: _________

MONDAY

DESCRIPTION	AMOUNT
TOTAL	

TUESDAY

DESCRIPTION	AMOUNT
TOTAL	

WEDNESDAY

DESCRIPTION	AMOUNT
TOTAL	

THURSDAY

DESCRIPTION	AMOUNT
TOTAL	

WEEKLY EXPENSES

FRIDAY

DESCRIPTION	AMOUNT
TOTAL	

SATURDAY

DESCRIPTION	AMOUNT
TOTAL	

SUNDAY

DESCRIPTION	AMOUNT
TOTAL	

NOTES

WEEKLY EXPENSES

MONTH:__________ WEEK:_________ BUDGET: _________

MONDAY

DESCRIPTION	AMOUNT
TOTAL	

TUESDAY

DESCRIPTION	AMOUNT
TOTAL	

WEDNESDAY

DESCRIPTION	AMOUNT
TOTAL	

THURSDAY

DESCRIPTION	AMOUNT
TOTAL	

WEEKLY EXPENSES

FRIDAY

DESCRIPTION	AMOUNT
TOTAL	

SATURDAY

DESCRIPTION	AMOUNT
TOTAL	

SUNDAY

DESCRIPTION	AMOUNT
TOTAL	

NOTES

WEEKLY EXPENSES

MONTH:__________ WEEK:_________ BUDGET: _________

MONDAY

DESCRIPTION	AMOUNT
TOTAL	

TUESDAY

DESCRIPTION	AMOUNT
TOTAL	

WEDNESDAY

DESCRIPTION	AMOUNT
TOTAL	

THURSDAY

DESCRIPTION	AMOUNT
TOTAL	

WEEKLY EXPENSES

FRIDAY

DESCRIPTION	AMOUNT
TOTAL	

SATURDAY

DESCRIPTION	AMOUNT
TOTAL	

SUNDAY

DESCRIPTION	AMOUNT
TOTAL	

NOTES

WEEKLY EXPENSES

MONTH:__________ WEEK:_________ BUDGET: _________

MONDAY

DESCRIPTION	AMOUNT
TOTAL	

TUESDAY

DESCRIPTION	AMOUNT
TOTAL	

WEDNESDAY

DESCRIPTION	AMOUNT
TOTAL	

THURSDAY

DESCRIPTION	AMOUNT
TOTAL	

WEEKLY EXPENSES

FRIDAY

DESCRIPTION	AMOUNT
TOTAL	

SATURDAY

DESCRIPTION	AMOUNT
TOTAL	

SUNDAY

DESCRIPTION	AMOUNT
TOTAL	

NOTES

MONTHLY BUDGET

MONTH:__________________ **BUDGET:**_______________

INCOME	AMOUNT
SOURCE 1:	
SOURCE 2:	
OTHER INCOME:	
TOTAL	

BILLS TO BE PAID	DATE DUE	AMOUNT	PAID
	TOTAL		

MONTHLY BUDGET

OTHER EXPENSES	DATE	AMOUNT
TOTAL		

TOTAL INCOME	TOTAL EXPENSES	DIFFERENCE

WEEKLY EXPENSES

MONTH:__________ WEEK:_________ BUDGET: _________

MONDAY

DESCRIPTION	AMOUNT
TOTAL	

TUESDAY

DESCRIPTION	AMOUNT
TOTAL	

WEDNESDAY

DESCRIPTION	AMOUNT
TOTAL	

THURSDAY

DESCRIPTION	AMOUNT
TOTAL	

WEEKLY EXPENSES

FRIDAY

DESCRIPTION	AMOUNT
TOTAL	

SATURDAY

DESCRIPTION	AMOUNT
TOTAL	

SUNDAY

DESCRIPTION	AMOUNT
TOTAL	

NOTES

WEEKLY EXPENSES

MONTH:__________ WEEK:_________ BUDGET: _________

MONDAY

DESCRIPTION	AMOUNT
TOTAL	

TUESDAY

DESCRIPTION	AMOUNT
TOTAL	

WEDNESDAY

DESCRIPTION	AMOUNT
TOTAL	

THURSDAY

DESCRIPTION	AMOUNT
TOTAL	

WEEKLY EXPENSES

FRIDAY

DESCRIPTION	AMOUNT
TOTAL	

SATURDAY

DESCRIPTION	AMOUNT
TOTAL	

SUNDAY

DESCRIPTION	AMOUNT
TOTAL	

NOTES

WEEKLY EXPENSES

MONTH:__________ WEEK:_________ BUDGET: _________

MONDAY

DESCRIPTION	AMOUNT
TOTAL	

TUESDAY

DESCRIPTION	AMOUNT
TOTAL	

WEDNESDAY

DESCRIPTION	AMOUNT
TOTAL	

THURSDAY

DESCRIPTION	AMOUNT
TOTAL	

WEEKLY EXPENSES

FRIDAY

DESCRIPTION	AMOUNT
TOTAL	

SATURDAY

DESCRIPTION	AMOUNT
TOTAL	

SUNDAY

DESCRIPTION	AMOUNT
TOTAL	

NOTES

WEEKLY EXPENSES

MONTH:__________ WEEK:_________ BUDGET: _________

MONDAY

DESCRIPTION	AMOUNT
TOTAL	

TUESDAY

DESCRIPTION	AMOUNT
TOTAL	

WEDNESDAY

DESCRIPTION	AMOUNT
TOTAL	

THURSDAY

DESCRIPTION	AMOUNT
TOTAL	

WEEKLY EXPENSES

FRIDAY

DESCRIPTION	AMOUNT
TOTAL	

SATURDAY

DESCRIPTION	AMOUNT
TOTAL	

SUNDAY

DESCRIPTION	AMOUNT
TOTAL	

NOTES

MONTHLY BUDGET

MONTH:__________________ **BUDGET:**_______________

INCOME		AMOUNT
SOURCE 1:		
SOURCE 2:		
OTHER INCOME:		
	TOTAL	

BILLS TO BE PAID	DATE DUE	AMOUNT	PAID
	TOTAL		

MONTHLY BUDGET

OTHER EXPENSES	DATE	AMOUNT
TOTAL		

TOTAL INCOME	TOTAL EXPENSES	DIFFERENCE

WEEKLY EXPENSES

MONTH:__________ WEEK:_________ BUDGET: _________

MONDAY

DESCRIPTION	AMOUNT
TOTAL	

TUESDAY

DESCRIPTION	AMOUNT
TOTAL	

WEDNESDAY

DESCRIPTION	AMOUNT
TOTAL	

THURSDAY

DESCRIPTION	AMOUNT
TOTAL	

WEEKLY EXPENSES

FRIDAY

DESCRIPTION	AMOUNT
TOTAL	

SATURDAY

DESCRIPTION	AMOUNT
TOTAL	

SUNDAY

DESCRIPTION	AMOUNT
TOTAL	

NOTES

WEEKLY EXPENSES

MONTH:__________ WEEK:_________ BUDGET: _________

MONDAY

DESCRIPTION	AMOUNT
TOTAL	

TUESDAY

DESCRIPTION	AMOUNT
TOTAL	

WEDNESDAY

DESCRIPTION	AMOUNT
TOTAL	

THURSDAY

DESCRIPTION	AMOUNT
TOTAL	

WEEKLY EXPENSES

FRIDAY

DESCRIPTION	AMOUNT
TOTAL	

SATURDAY

DESCRIPTION	AMOUNT
TOTAL	

SUNDAY

DESCRIPTION	AMOUNT
TOTAL	

NOTES

WEEKLY EXPENSES

MONTH:__________ WEEK:_________ BUDGET: _________

MONDAY

DESCRIPTION	AMOUNT
TOTAL	

TUESDAY

DESCRIPTION	AMOUNT
TOTAL	

WEDNESDAY

DESCRIPTION	AMOUNT
TOTAL	

THURSDAY

DESCRIPTION	AMOUNT
TOTAL	

WEEKLY EXPENSES

FRIDAY

DESCRIPTION	AMOUNT
TOTAL	

SATURDAY

DESCRIPTION	AMOUNT
TOTAL	

SUNDAY

DESCRIPTION	AMOUNT
TOTAL	

NOTES

WEEKLY EXPENSES

MONTH:__________ WEEK:_________ BUDGET: _________

MONDAY

DESCRIPTION	AMOUNT
TOTAL	

TUESDAY

DESCRIPTION	AMOUNT
TOTAL	

WEDNESDAY

DESCRIPTION	AMOUNT
TOTAL	

THURSDAY

DESCRIPTION	AMOUNT
TOTAL	

WEEKLY EXPENSES

FRIDAY

DESCRIPTION	AMOUNT
TOTAL	

SATURDAY

DESCRIPTION	AMOUNT
TOTAL	

SUNDAY

DESCRIPTION	AMOUNT
TOTAL	

NOTES

MONTHLY BUDGET

MONTH:__________________ **BUDGET:**_______________

INCOME	AMOUNT
SOURCE 1:	
SOURCE 2:	
OTHER INCOME:	
TOTAL	

BILLS TO BE PAID	DATE DUE	AMOUNT	PAID
	TOTAL		

MONTHLY BUDGET

OTHER EXPENSES	DATE	AMOUNT
	TOTAL	

TOTAL INCOME	TOTAL EXPENSES	DIFFERENCE

WEEKLY EXPENSES

MONTH:__________ WEEK:_________ BUDGET: _________

MONDAY

DESCRIPTION	AMOUNT
TOTAL	

TUESDAY

DESCRIPTION	AMOUNT
TOTAL	

WEDNESDAY

DESCRIPTION	AMOUNT
TOTAL	

THURSDAY

DESCRIPTION	AMOUNT
TOTAL	

WEEKLY EXPENSES

FRIDAY

DESCRIPTION	AMOUNT
TOTAL	

SATURDAY

DESCRIPTION	AMOUNT
TOTAL	

SUNDAY

DESCRIPTION	AMOUNT
TOTAL	

NOTES

WEEKLY EXPENSES

MONTH:__________ WEEK:_________ BUDGET: _________

MONDAY

DESCRIPTION	AMOUNT
TOTAL	

TUESDAY

DESCRIPTION	AMOUNT
TOTAL	

WEDNESDAY

DESCRIPTION	AMOUNT
TOTAL	

THURSDAY

DESCRIPTION	AMOUNT
TOTAL	

WEEKLY EXPENSES

FRIDAY

DESCRIPTION	AMOUNT
TOTAL	

SATURDAY

DESCRIPTION	AMOUNT
TOTAL	

SUNDAY

DESCRIPTION	AMOUNT
TOTAL	

NOTES

WEEKLY EXPENSES

MONTH:__________ WEEK:_________ BUDGET: _________

MONDAY

DESCRIPTION	AMOUNT
TOTAL	

TUESDAY

DESCRIPTION	AMOUNT
TOTAL	

WEDNESDAY

DESCRIPTION	AMOUNT
TOTAL	

THURSDAY

DESCRIPTION	AMOUNT
TOTAL	

WEEKLY EXPENSES

FRIDAY

DESCRIPTION	AMOUNT
TOTAL	

SATURDAY

DESCRIPTION	AMOUNT
TOTAL	

SUNDAY

DESCRIPTION	AMOUNT
TOTAL	

NOTES

WEEKLY EXPENSES

MONTH:__________ WEEK:_________ BUDGET: _________

MONDAY

DESCRIPTION	AMOUNT
TOTAL	

TUESDAY

DESCRIPTION	AMOUNT
TOTAL	

WEDNESDAY

DESCRIPTION	AMOUNT
TOTAL	

THURSDAY

DESCRIPTION	AMOUNT
TOTAL	

WEEKLY EXPENSES

FRIDAY

DESCRIPTION	AMOUNT
TOTAL	

SATURDAY

DESCRIPTION	AMOUNT
TOTAL	

SUNDAY

DESCRIPTION	AMOUNT
TOTAL	

NOTES

www.ingramcontent.com/pod-product-compliance
Lightning Source LLC
Chambersburg PA
CBHW081310070526
44578CB00006B/827
* 9 7 8 1 9 5 3 5 5 7 5 4 4 *